1000
CORNISH PLACE NAMES
EXPLAINED

by

JULYAN HOLMES

Illustrations by Laura Rowe

Published by Dyllansow Truran, Truran Publications, Trewolsta, Trewirgie, Redruth, Kernow.

DEDICATION

Dhe'm caradow, Loveday, may cafaf kerensa, kennerth ha govynek.

Copyright © 1983

I.S.B.N. No. 0-907566-76-6

Printed in Great Britain by BPCC Wheatons Ltd, Exeter

ACKNOWLEDGEMENT

It would have been quite impossible to compile this book were it not for the work of scholars such as Henderson, Gover, Pool, Morton Nance, etc... My thanks go to these and Oliver Padel and others whose advice was invaluable but who should on no account be held responsible for any errors.

FOREWORD

Cornwall's strange, mellifluous place-names give it a flavour quite different from English counties. Many must wonder where they all came from.

This book is designed to help not only the bewildered stranger but also the born Cornishman who may have taken them for granted since childhood.

Our abandoned engine-houses and deserted coves, so beloved by romantics, are a constant reminder of a way of life now gone, when copper, fish and tin gave thousands of Cornishmen and women their livelihood. In just the same way, once you know the secret, our place-names open the door to a new language and, in fact, to a whole Celtic civilisation which is the true heritage of *KERNOW*.

Renewed awareness of Cornwall's submerged identity has led to a growing interest in its celtic heritage. Every year, more and more people are introduced to the Cornish language. Both in and out of school. While not all will go on to speak it fluently, they naturally wish to make sense of those words of Cornish that we all use every day - - - - words which many bear as their surnames.

For place-names are as much part of the language as the words for 'butter' or 'cheese'. In fact, if you browse through the pages of this book, you will soon find that you have learnt a dozen or so words and their meanings.

Out of the thousands of Cornish place-names, I have only been able to include one thousand, mainly the names of towns, villages and farms, with a sprinkling of coastal names and a few others of special interest.

Although the vast majority of farms are named in Cornish, there are, for historical reasons, some in French, many in English (and Old English) and even some with a little Latin! The only English names included are those which might be mistaken for Cornish.

Inevitably, in such a long list, every name cannot always be fully explained: sometimes they contain forgotten or unrecognized words but, much more often, specially in those beginning *Bos, Car, Lan, Res* or *Tre*, the second part is an old Celtic personal name. Such names were given a thousand or more years ago and probably had no more meaning to the medieval Cornish-speaker than does the name Alfred to a present-day Englishman.

Some better-known examples, of personal names, enough to give the 'feel' of them, can be found on page 11.

A LITTLE HISTORY

The Cornish language is directly descended from the Celtic of ancient Gaul and pre-Roman Britain, so we can say that it has been spoken here for more than two thousand years. Its closest relatives are Welsh and Breton and it has a kinship with Irish, Scottish and Manx Gaelic.

After the Roman Empire collapsed, shortly after 400 AD, English (or Saxon) settlers from North Germany began to overrun the island. By 800 AD, the British language was confined to Cornwall, Wales, Cumbria, South Scotland and Brittany (where it had been taken by emigrants from the south west).

During the ninth and tenth centuries, Cornwall fell under the sway of the powerful kings of Wessex. Saxons settled in the north and east, especially north of Bude, where Cornish names are scarce. Outside this area, English -*ton* added to Cornish names, marks their colonial centres, but the Cornish people continued to use their own language.

At about this time, Cornish and Welsh began to go their own separate ways, though, even today, many of our place-names are instantly recognizable to a Welshman. This is even more true for Breton since that language remained identical for centuries more. Shortly after, the Normans came, adding French to the language mix. Old Cornish was transformed into Middle Cornish. The most obvious change was of *t* into *s* in many words, such as *cuit* a - wood (compare Welsh *coed*) which became *cos*.

Throughout the Middle Ages, Cornish retreated westwards under the pressure of English. In 1400, Cornish could have been heard everywhere west of a line from Tintagel to Looe. By the time of the Reformation (c. 1540), it had disappeared east of Bodmin, though, further west, English was hardly known outside the towns.

Up to then, religious or 'miracle' plays, performed in Cornish in a *Plen an Gwary* or open-air theatre, had done much to keep the language alive. The new Anglican churchmen did not approve of them and they fell into disuse. When the pro-Catholic Prayerbook Rebellion of 1549 was defeated, many Cornishmen (whose fathers had twice marched against English armies) were 'persuaded' to adopt English ways. History was to prove that learning English did little to improve the lot of the Cornish peasant!

Even so, long after this, some Cornishmen so resented the foreigners that they would reply to an enquiry in English,
"My ny vynnaf cows sawsnek" "I will not speak English"!

Nevertheless another century saw Cornish driven west of Truro, where, its literature forgotten, it lingered on the lips of fishermen until about 1800, and faded from the scene, as did the last chough a century or so later, on the very edge of the Atlantic cliffs.

Fortunately the seeds of revival had already been sown, and, after a period of ignominy, Cornish is again on the lips of Cornishmen.

The Spelling of Place Names

At the time when most Cornish literature was being composed, roughly between 1400 and 1600, the spelling was at least as regular as contemporary English, but, as Cornish was abandoned bit by bit, so the spelling became more and more erratic.

As a general rule, the *later* the date of the record, the *worse* the spelling. For that reason *it is no use looking in a dictionary for the meaning of a traditional place-name.* It is vital to look at older spellings before trying to interpret them.

Apart from the irregular and anglicised spellings, some coastal names have even been re-spelt by chart-makers as Welsh! There are several changes in pronunciation which are reflected in writing. Because the language passed out of use later in the west than in the east, names are preserved in an older form on Bodmin Moor than at Land's End.

Penquite, *Pen cuit,* is found further west as Pencoose, *Pencoos,* with the same meaning, "end of the wood". An even later development turned *Pen* into *Pedn* and *Crom* (curved) into *crobben.* This affected several other words as well.

Besides these historical changes, there are also some regular ones caused by Celtic grammar. Known as 'mutations', these rules mean that the first letter of some words in certain set positions must change into another.

By these rules, B and M both become V, D becomes Th (strictly Dh), C and K become G, G becomes W or else disappears, P becomes B and T becomes D. In place-names only, F will appear as V, and S as Z.

These changes are found with feminine nouns after *An* (the) and with other words placed immediately after feminine nouns, (all nouns in Cornish are classed as either masculine or feminine).

For example, 'The Upper Farm' in Cornish is *An dre wartha,* made up of *An+tre+gwartha.*

Another point of interest is that many words ending *-ow* are plurals.

Finally, since these names were passed on by word of mouth from generation to generation, they often become distorted in ways which do not follow any rules.

Some words are mistaken for one another; in particular there is a tendancy for many words to end up as Tre, Pol or Lan. Also, R and N are both liable to become L, especially at the beginning of a name, while R and S are often interchanged in middle position. C (K) is also liable to be exchanged for T, while amongst vowel sounds, perhaps the most significant alteration is that of *yr* (ir) and *er* to *ar* at the beginning of a name, as with all those starting Car- (which were originally Ker-).

Other examples of such changes can be spotted in the word-lists on pages 10-52, where I have put together many of the commonest words found in place-names with some of the strange forms thay have taken.

A LITTLE GRAMMAR

A casual glance shows that Cornish is not a bit like English. The words are unfamiliar, and so is the grammar, which is in many ways more like French than English.

In particular, Cornish, like French, generally puts the adjective (or describing word) after the noun, instead of in front of it as in English. In the name *Menhyr*, (long stone), the Cornish words *men* (stone) and *hyr* (long) are in the opposite order to the English.

In the same way, where English says Johnston (John's town), Cornish says *Trejowan* (where *Tre* means 'town').

Others describing parts of a name also follow the main noun: in the name Rose-an-Grouse *(Ros an grows)* meaning 'Cross Heath', the Cornish reads word for word "heath (of) the cross". (The word 'of' is not needed in the Cornish.)

Of course there are exceptions, since, just as in French, some adjectives are frequently placed before the noun. The main ones are the colours *gwyn*, white, *ruth*, red, *gwer*, green and *melen*, yellow, plus *hen*, old, *ber*, short, *hyr*, long and *mol*, bare.

Pronunciation

In nearly every case the traditional pronunciation of place-names still points to its meaning, and it is a great pity when the accent is misplaced.

Just as in English one says "Longstone" with the stress on *Long*, so Cornish stresses the same word in "Menheere" *(Men hyr)*, with the stress on "heere". For this reason most two-syllable place-names are stressed on the second part, while longer names are stressed on the next-to-last syllable.

The common pattern can be remembered by thinking of the words "Resign" and "Tremendous" (both of which could easily appear on a Cornish map).

Most exceptions are equally logical: Hendra, Gwendreath, *Gwyndreth*, Harlyn, *Hyrlyn*, etc., all stressed on the first part, or Menadew, *Meneth du*, Canakey, *Carn an ky*, etc., all stressed on the last part. It is always the describing element that is emphasised - that is the part of the name which distinguishes that particular hill, farm or beach.

One personal name at least was also stressed on the last syllable: Kenhorn, which is formed in Polkinghorne, and Linkinhorne, and explains the irregular pronunciation of these two names.

Finally beware of traps like Tregony (NOT Tre-goaney but Tregny) which is due to contraction of a longer word. Luxulyan too, is very often mispronounced: the middle *u* represents the sound 'i' as it often does in the Cornish language so that the name rhymes with 'million'. After reading this introduction and looking up the meaning of Cardinham, nobody will dream of calling that place Carding'm !

Crantock

1

Common Cornish Words as found in Place-Names

(dictionary spellings in Italics)

Alls, alt, halt	*als*	- cliff
An	*an*	- the
Bal	*bal*	- mine
Bar	*bar*	- top
Beagle, biggal, bugle	*1. begel. 2. bugel*	- 1. small hill. 2. shepherd
Bell	*bell (pell)*	- far
Bo, bos, bod, be, bis, bus	*bos*	- dwelling
Bowgie	*bowjy*	- cowshed
Brane	*bran*	- crow
Bray, brea	*bre*	- hill
Braze, brawze	*bras*	- big
Burn,	*bryn*	- hill
Car, caer	*ker*	- walled village
Carn, can	*carn*	- rock-pile
Carow	*carow*	- stag
Carrack, carrag, carrick	*carrek*	- rock
Che, chi, chy, ch-	*chy*	- house
Coose, cos, coys, cus, cut	*cos*	- a wood
Coath, coth	*coth*	- old
Craze	*cres*	- middle
Creeg, creek, crig, creet	*cruk*	- mound, barrow
Crows	*crows*	- cross
Deen, din, dun	*dyn*	- fort
Dennis, dinas	*dynas*	- fort
-dew, -due	*du*	- black
Dour, dower	*dowr*	- water
Dow, do, du	*deu* (or fem. *dyw*)	- two
-dra, -drea	*dra (tre)*	- home
-dreath	*dreth (treth)*	- beach
Drennick, drinnick	*dreynek*	- thorny
-drizzick, -drisack	*dreysek*	- brambly
Eglos, -iglas	*eglos*	- church

En	*an*	- the
Ennis, innis, enys	*enys*	- island, dislocated place
Fenton, fenter	*fenten*	- a spring
Garrack, garrick	*garrek (carrek)*	- rock
Gazick	*gasek (casek)*	- mare
Gear	*ger (ker)*	- walled village
Gelly, gilly	*gelly (kelly)*	- grove
-gett, -gus, -goose	*Gos (cos)*	- a wood
-gey	*jy (chy)*	- house
gew	*gew (kew)*	- enclosed field
Gon, goon, gun	*gun*	- downs
Gooth	*goth*	- goose
Goth	*goth (coth)*	- old
Gove	*gof*	- smith
Gover	*gover*	- stream
-graze	*gres (cres)*	- middle
-grean, green, grain	*grun*	- gravel*
Greeb, gribba, gribben	*gryb (cryb) gryben*	- crest
Grey	*gre*	- flock, herd
grows	*grows (crows)*	- cross
Gweal	*gwel*	- cultivated field
Gwen, -gwin, -gwidden	*gwyn*	- white
Hal, hale, hall, haul, hole	*hal*	- moor
Har, her, -heer, -hyr	*hyr*	- long
Helligan, hellick	*helyk, helygen*	- willow(s)
Hels, helles	*hellys (hen lys)*	- old court
Hen	*hen*	- old
Henver	*henforth*	- old road
Ince, innis	*enys*	- island, isolated place
Kelly, killy	*kelly*	- grove
kernick	*kernek*	- corner
Kestle	*kestel*	- castle, village
Kie, key	*ky*	- dog
La, le, lan, lans, lant	*nans*	- valley
Lan	*lan*	- holy enclosure

3

-lay, -lee,	*legh*	- flat rock
-laze	*las (glas)*	- green/blue
Les	*lys*	- mud
Les, lis	*lys*	- court, palace
Lid, lis, loose, luz	*los*	- grey, hoary
Lidden, lin, lyn	*lyn*	- pool, lake
Loe, looe	*logh*	- creek, inlet
Main, mayne, mean, men, min	*men*	- stone
Mellan, Molin, Bolin-	*melyn*	- mill
Min	*myn*	- edge
Mor	*mor*	- sea
Mul,	*mol*	- bare
Nan, nam, nance, nans, nant	*nans*	- valley
Nare	*an arth (garth)*	- the heights
-newth, nouth, noweth, nowth	*noweth*	- new
Ninnes	*an enys*	- the island, isolated place
Noon, un, owen	*an un (gun)*	- the downs
Ogo	*ogo (gogo)*	- cave
Owles	*als*	- cliff
Par, (parn)	*porth*	- cove, landing-place
Parc, park	*park*	- field, close
-parrett, parva, parvath	*perveth*	- inner, middle
Pedn, pen, pe, p-	*pen*	- head, end, top
-pean	*byghan*	- little
Pit, pits	*pyt* or plural *pyttys*	- pit, pits
Pol, poll	*poll* (often for *porth*)	- pool
Pons, ponds, pols, pont	*pons*	- bridge
Porth, port, per, pr-, pol	*porth*	- cove, landing-place
Praze	*pras*	- meadow
-quin, -quidden	*gwyn*	- white
-quite	*cos*	- wood
Re, red, res, ris, ros, -rice	*res* (often for *ros*)	- ford
Reen, -ridden, -ryn	*ryn*	- slope
Reeth	*ryth* (sometimes =*ruth*)	- free
Rose	*ros* (often for *res*)	- heath, or promontory
Ruth	*ruth*	- red

4

Scawen, scow, -scoe	*scawen, plural scaw*	- eldertree(s)
-sew, -sue	*du*	- black
Sparnon, spearn	*spernen, plural spern*	- thorntree(s)
-stain	*sten*	- tin
Sten, stephen, St.	*stum*	- bend
Tal, tol	*tal*	- brow, 'next to'
Tol, toll	*tol (often for tal)*	- hole
Todden, ton, tane	*ton*	- grassland
Towan	*towan*	- dune
Treath	*treth*	- beach, strand
Tre, trev, tor, tr-	*tre*	- farm, village
Trem, tren	*tre'n (tre an)*	- farm of the
Tres	*ros (confused with ros)*	- heath or promontory
Ty	*chy*	- house
-va	*va*	- place
-vadden, -van	*van (ban)*	- a height
Vear, veor	*vur (mur)*	- great
Vellan, vellyn, valley	*velyn (melyn)*	- mill
-vena, -venner	*veneth (meneth)*	- hill
Venton	*fenten*	- spring
-vose, voose	*fos*	- dyke
-vrane	*vran (bran)*	- crow (sometimes personal name)
-vraze	*vras (bras)*	- big
-vrea, -vra	*vre (bre)*	- hill
Vounder	*vownder (Bownder)*	- the cattle-track lane
-warne	*wern*	- (gwern)
Wartha	*wartha (gwartha)*	- higher
-wen, -widden, -win, -wyn	*wyn (gwyn)*	- white
Wheal	*whel*	- mine-working
-wins, -wint	*wyns (gwyns)*	- wind
-withen	*wedhen (gwedhen)*	- tree (but see main list)
-woolas	*woles (goles)*	- lower
-woon	*un (gun)*	- downs
-zance	*sans*	- holy
Zawn	*saun*	- cleft in cliffs

Jamaica Inn, Bolventor.

FIELDS AND MINES

The main list in this book does not include many fieldnames, but, since many of these survive, often used for housing estates, and also for the benefit of those looking at old records, here is a small sample.

Fieldnames :

Croft	*croft*	- small holding
Dor, doar	*dor*	- ground, small plot
Erow, ali	*erow.*	- acre
Gew, gue	*gew (kew)*	- close, usually near farm-house
Gweal	*gwel*	- open cultivated field
Lean	*lyn*	- strip or stitch
Park	*park*	- field or close
Praze	*pras*	- meadow
Vithan	*vuthyn (buthyn*	- meadow

Most of these words may be followed by any of the descriptive elements in the above list, by the name of the owner, Croft Pascoe, Park Davey, etc., or by such phrases as these : (The word *an* is often ommited.)

(an)	Bannel	*banal*	- broom
	Beath	*beth*	- grave
	Bowen	*bowen*	- beef or steer
	Bucca	*bucca*	- spirit, (later scarecrow)
	Chapel	*Chapel*	- chapel
	Dandrea	*yn dan an dre*	- below the farm or town
(an)	Darras	*darras*	- door
	Dodnan	*donnen (tonnen)*	- piece of turf
	Drain	*dreyn*	- thorns
	Drea	*dre (tre)*	- home-field
	Friglas	*forth eglos*	- church-way
	Grambla	*gromlegh (cromlegh)*	- cromlegh, stone monument
	Grengy	*grunjy*	- grange
	Gwith	*gwyth*	- trees
	Hor	*horth*	- ram
	Ithan (nathan)	*eythen*	- furze, gorse
	Intranthewhenver	*yntra'n dhyw henforth*	- between the two old roads
(an)	Kine	*keyn*	- back, ridge
	Mo	*mogh*	- pigs

Noath	noth	- naked
Noonpoocas, onypokis	an un buccyas	- downs of the ghosts or spirits
Panesse	panes	- parsnips
Peeth	pyth	- well
Pillas	pyllas	- a kind of oats, once staple diet
Skeber	skyber	- barn
Sowle	sowl	- stubble, thatch
Sperris	spedhes	- briars
Stenor	stenor	- tinner
Tarow	tarow	- bull
Tubman	tomen	- hummock
Vaze	a-ves	- outer
Vor	forth	- road
Vorn	forn	- furnace
Weeth	wyth (gwyth)	- watercourse
Yeat	yet	- gate

The word *conna* (neck), used for narrow fields, also occurs in the common nick-name Crackagodna *(crak y gonna),* for verry steep ones.

Mine Names :

A prospector's patch or 'bound' was christened in much the same way as a field. Actual mine-names usually begin with Wheal *(whel),* a works, or Bal which usually means a larger conglomeration of mining setts. These names very often completed with the name of the land-owner, the 'adventurer' (entrepreneur) or their ladies. Because Wheal remained in fashion throughout the boom years of mining, many such names are half English, some deliberate puns like Wheal Prosper, Wheal Speed, or Charles Dickens' Wheal Do'em', which accurately reflects the attitude of some adventurers to their investors.

A few Cornish names recorded for mine-works, some of them very old, are listed below:

Crease an Pocket	*cres an pocket*	- Middle of the Pocket
Hagarowal	*hager awel*	- Fowl Weather
Coffenoola	*coffen ula*	- Open-work of the Owl
Wheal an Cleath (Clay)	*w. an cleth*	- Ditch Mine
Wheal an Howl	*w. an howl*	- Sun Mine
Wheal an Stearan	*w. an steren*	- The Star Mine
Wheal Mehal	*w. Myghal*	- (St. Michael's Mine
Wheal Maria, Variah	*w. Marya, Varya*	- Mary's Mine
Wheal Perran	*w. Peran*	- (St) Perran's Mine
Wheal 'Tis Gentle	*w. an dusjentyl*	- Gentleman's Mine

Naturally Wheal may be followed by any of the descriptive words or phrases in the above two lists - or of course many others.

St. Breward Church

A

Adjewednack	*Aswy-wynek*	- Gap + personal name
Aire	*Arth*	- High place
Atarnun	*Altarnon*	- St Non's altar
Amalveor, -widden	*Amal vur, wyn*	- Great (or white) slope
Anderton		- Under (lower) farm (Eng.)
Andrewartha	*An dre-wartha*	- The higher farm
Angarrack, Angarrick	*An garrek*	- The rock
Angear	*An ger*	- The fortified village
Angew	*An gew*	- The close
Angrowse	*An grows*	- The cross
Anhay	*An hay*	- The hedge or close
Anjarden	*An jarden*	- The garden
Anvoase	*An vos*	- The dyke
Ardevora (Veor)	*Ardevran (Vur)*	- The (great) farm on the watery land
Argal	*Argel*	- At the place of retreat
Asparagus Island		- (Eng.) (from wild plant)
August Rock	*?Men Ogas*	- possibly 'The near rock'
Ayr	*Arth*	- High place

B

Bake		- (Eng.) 'Back', ridge
Baldhu	*Bal du*	- Black mine
Ball	*Bal*	- Mine
Balleswidden	*Bal-lys-wyn*	- The mine of the white mud
Banns	*Bans*	- High place
Barbican (Looe)	*Bar vyghan*	- Little summit
Bareppa (see Berepper)		
Bargoes, Bargus	*Bargos*	- Summit of wood
Barncoose	*Bron cos*	- Wood hill
Barnoon	*Bar' n un*	- Summit of the downs
Barrimaylor	*Merther Maelor*	- Burial-place of St Maylor
Barriper (see Berepper)		
Beara, berah		- Grove (Old English)

Benallack	*Banathlek*	- Broombrake	
Berepper		- Fine retreat (French) 'Beau-repere'	
Berry		- Old hill-fort (Eng.)	
Biggal	*Begel*	- Hummock	
Bissoe	*Besow*	- Birch-trees	
Blisland		- Celtic word +(Eng.) land	
Blowing-house		- From old tin foundry (Eng.)	

Place names beginning BO, BOD, BOS, BE, etc., (also CAR, TRE and LAN) are often completed with name of the founder of the settlement.

These names are quite unfamiliar to us today. They resemble the names of characters in Old Welsh legend and history and are derived from names like Caratacus, current in Britain before the Romans came. Often we can not be certain about them for they may occur only once, but just a few can be found in their original form amongst the names of slaves whose, manumissions were recorded in the 10th century in the 'Bodmin Gospels'.

Below are a few 'BOS' names where the second element is definitely a corrupt form of the founder's name :

Bejowan	—	*Dwelling of*	Ewein
Boconnoc	—		Conoc
Bodbrane	—		Bran
Bodiggo	—		Uuithgi (Gwithgy)
Bodilly	—		Ili
Bodithiel	—		Iudhael
Bodrigan	—		Rigan
Bogee, Bojea	—		Yuf
Bokenna	—		Ceneu
Bolenna, -now	—		......
Bolitho	—		......
Bollowal	—		?Lewhael
Boskennal	—		Cenwal
Bosmawgan	—		Maelcun
Bosworgey	—		Uuorci (Gorgy)
Bosworlas	—		Gorloes
Bottallack	—		Taloc
Botternell, Boturnal	—		......

Bodinick	*Bos-dynek*	- Fortified dwelling, or else the second part may be a personal name, as, definitely, at St Tudy.
Bodmin	*Bos-venegh*	- Originally 'dwelling of the sanctuary,' later, 'of monks'.
Bodwen	*Bos-wyn*	- White dwelling
Bolankan		- ?Possibly dwelling by defile
Bolingey	*Melynjy*	- Mill house
Bollogas	*Bos-logas*	- Dwelling of mice (or personal name)
Bolventor		- Bold Venture (Eng. field-name)
Bonallack	*Banathlek*	- Broombrake
Bonyalva	*Banathelva*	- Broom place
Borlase (-Vath)	*Burlas (Vargh)*	- Probably 'Green bank' (of Mark)
Boscarn, Boscarne	*Bos-carn*	- Dwelling by rock pile
Boscastle		- Botterel's castle (Eng.)
Boscawen	*?Bos-scawen*	- Dwelling of eldertree (or Gawen's dwelling)
Boscean	*Bos-seghan*	- Dwelling at dry spot
Boscreege	*Bos-cruk*	- Dwelling by mound or barrow
Bosence, Bosent	*Bos-syns*	- Dwelling of saints
Bosporthennis	*Bos-porth-enys*	- Dwelling at the entrance to the isolated place
Bostrase, Bostraze	*Bos-stras*	- Dwelling in low ground
Boswedden	*Bos-wyn*	- White dwelling
Boswin, Boswyn	*Bos-wyn*	- White dwelling
Botus fleming	*Bos-flumyes*	- Dwelling + obscure personal name
Bowdah		- Bend of wood (old English)
Bowden		- Curved hill (Eng.)
Bozion	*Bron-seghan*	- Breast of hill of dry spot
Bray	*Bre*	- Hill
Brea (Vean)	*Bre (vyghan)*	- (Little) hill
Breage		- Name of parish saint
Brendon		- Burnt hill (Eng.)
Brighton		- prob. Eng. 'Bright farm'
Brightor		- prob. Eng. 'Bright hill'
Browngelly	*Bryn-gelow*	- Hill + unknown word
Brown willy	*?Bron wynlegh*	- ?Hill of white flat stone
Brynn	*Bryn*	- Hill
Budock	*Budhek*	- Name of Saint
Burlorne	*Bos-elowen*	- Dwelling of elmtree (or personal name)

Burncoose	Broncos	- Hill or top of wood
Burngullow	Bron-golow	- Bright hill ('hill of light')
Burniere	Bry hyr	- Long hill
Burras	Ber-res	- Short ford
Burraton		- Boar or hill town (Eng.)
Bury		- Old hill-fort (Eng.)

Wheal Drea Engine House, St. Just

C

Cadgwith	*Caswyth*	- Bushes (poss. Personal name)
Cadsonbury		- Hill-fort at Cadoc's farm (Eng.)
Cadythew	*Carrek Dhu*	- Black rock
Caer Bran	*Ker-vran*	- Fortified village of Bran (pers. name)
Cairo	*Kerrow*	- Camps, fortified villages
Calamansak		- poss. 'Retreat on small mound'
Calenick	*Kelyneck*	- Hollybushes
Callenowth	*Kelly-gnowek*	- Nut grove
Camborne	*Cambron*	- Curve of the hill
Camelford		- Probably 'Curved Estuary' Eng. Ford.
Canakey	*Carn an Ky*	- Rock-pile of the dog
Canaglaze	*Carn-glas*	- Blue-green rock-pile
Cannalidgey	*Canol Ysy*	- Middle (of parish) of Issey
Caragloose	*Carrek Los*	- Grey Rock
Carbis	*Carbons*	- Cart-bridge
Carclaze	*Cruk-glas*	- Blue mound or burrow
Cardew	*ker-dhu*	- Black hill-fort
Candinham	*Ker-Dhynan*	- Hill-fort or Dinan (pers. name)
Cargenwen	*Ker-Genwyn*	- Hill-fort of Kenwyn
Cargreen	*Carrek-run*	- Seal rock
Carleen, Carleon	*Ker-leghyon*	- Hill fort
Carlidnack, Carlinick		- Hill-fort & personal name
Carloggas	*Ker-logas*	- Hill-fort of mice (or else pers. name)
Carn, Carne	*Carn*	- Rock-pile
Carnaquidden	*Kernek-wyn*	- White rock-pile (or nook)
Carnbargus	*Carn Bargos*	- 'Carn' (rock pile- of kite
Carn Base	*Carn Bas*	- Shallow carn
Carn Boel	*Carn Mol*	- Bald, bare carn
Carn Clew, Clough	*Carn Clugh*	- possible 'Crag carn'
Carn Du	*Carn Du*	- Black carn
Carnewas	*Carn hewas*	- Carn of summer pasture
Carnglaze	*Carn glas*	- Grey rock
Carnglooze	*Carrek-los*	- Grey rock
Carn Haut, Hot	*Carn hot*	- Hat-shaped carn

Carnkie	*Carn Ky*	- Dog carn
Carnmarth	*Carn Margh*	- Mark's carn
Carnmenellis	*Carn-menelys*	- Rocks piled like sheaves
Carnon		- Poss. Small Carn
Carnsew	*Carn-du*	- Black carn
Carnsmerry	*Carn-ros-mur*	- Carn of the great heath
Carnyorth	*Carn-yorgh*	- Roebuck carn or rockpile
Carrack Gladden	*Carrek-lan*	- Rock on the bank
Carracks (The)	*Kerrygy*	- The rocks (Eng. plural)
Carrag-a-pilez	*Carrek-an-pyllas*	- The rock of oats (pillas)
Carrick Du	*Carrek Dhu*	- Black Rock
Carrick Luz	*Carrek Los*	- Grey rock
Carrick Nath	*Carrek Nath*	- Puffin rock
Carrick Roads		- Roadstead or achorage of the rock
Carthew	*Ker-dhu*	- Black hill-fort
Cartuther	*Cruk Tudher*	- Mound or burrow of Teudar (per. name)
Carvannel	*Ker-vanathel*	- Hill-fort of broom
Carvean	*Ker-vyghan*	- Little hill-fort
Carveddras	*Ker-Vedras*	- Hill-fort of Modred (pers. name)
Carvinack		- Stony hill-fort or Gwinoc's fort
Carwen	*Ker-wyn*	- White, or Gwyn's hill-fort
Carworgie		- Hill-fort of Gorgi
Carwythenack		- Hill-fort of Gwethenoc
Castle-an-Dinas	*Castel-an-dynas*	- Castle (a duplicated name since 'an dynas' means 'the fort')
Castle Canyke	*Castel Keynek*	- Conoc's castle
Castle Dore	*? Castel Dour*	- Perhaps 'severe castle'
Castle Gotha	*Castel Gothow*	- possibly 'Geese Castle'
Castle Wary		- possibly 'Castle of the playing-place'
Catchfrench		- Free hunting (French) 'Chasse-franche'
Chapel Amble		- named from its builder, Charles Rashleigh. Its old name was porth (or Poll) Mur, the great cove.
Chasewater	*(Dour an chas)*	- (Eng.) stream in hunting-ground
Chenall, Chenhale	*Chy an hal*	- House on the moor
Chenhalls	*- an als*	- House on the cliff
Chenoweth	*- noweth*	- New House

Chipponds	- *pons*	- Bridge House
Chiverton	*Chy war'n ton*	- House on the grassland
Choon, Choone	*Chy-un*	- House on the downs
Chun	*Chy-un*	- House on the downs
Chyandour	*Chy an dowr*	- House of the water or stream
Chyanvounder	*Chy an vownder*	- House of the lane
Chybucca	*Chybucca*	- Ghost or spirit house
Chycarne(e)	*carn*	- Carn (rock pile) house
Chycoose	*cos*	- Wood house
Chygwidden		- House of Uuorguin
Chyngwith	*Chy'n gwyth*	- House of the trees
Chykembro	*Chy-Kembro*	- House of Welshman
Chynhale	*Chy'n hal*	- House on the moor
Chynoweth	*Chy noweth*	- New house
-pons	*-pons*	- Bridge house
-praze	*-pras*	- Meadow house
-reen	*-ryn*	- Hillside house
-rose	*-ros*	- Heath house
Chysauster	*Chy-Salvester*	- Silvester's house
Chytan	*Chy war'n ton*	- House on the grassland
-todden	*Chy'n ton*	- House on the grassland
Chyvarton	*Chy'n ton*	- House on the grassland
Chywoon(e)	*Chy-un*	- Downs house
Cleave		- Cliff (Eng.)
Clennick, Clinnick	*Kelynek*	- Hollybushes
Clodgy	*Clafjy*	- Leaper-house, hospital
Coldharbour		- (Eng.) Field-name
Coldrennick, Coldrinnick	*Kyldreynek*	- Thorny back or ridge
Coldvreath	*Kelly-vryth*	- Speckléd grove
Colquite	*Kyl-cos*	- Back of the wood
Colvannick		- ?Prominent hill
Colvennor	*Kyl-veneth*	- Back of the hill
Come-to-good		- (Eng.) Probably nickname for field
Comfort		- ?(Eng.) ? Coombe, 'valley', ford
Comprigney	*Gwel Cloghprennyer*	- Gallowtrees field
Condurrow		- Poss. Junction of waters

Connor Downs		- From personal name
Coosebean	*Cos byghan*	- Little wood
Coosewartha	*Cos-wartha*	- Upper wood
Costislost		- (Eng.- Nickname for poor field
Cornakee, Cornakey	*Carn an Ky*	- Carn or rock pile of the dog
Cowyjack		- Sheltered place
Crane	*Ker-vran*	- Hillfort of Bran (pers. name) or crow
Crankan		- Hillfort & personal name
Creak-a-vose	*Cruk an fos*	- Mound or barrow of the dyke
Creegbrawse	*Cruk bras*	- Great mound or barrow
Cregoe	*Crugow*	- Barrows or mounds
Cribba	*Crybow*	- Crests
Crift		- Croft, small-holding
Crigmurrian	*Cruk Meryan*	- Merien's mound or barrow
Croft an Creeg	*Croft an cruk*	- Croft (small holding) of the barrow
Croft an Growse	*Croft an grows*	- of the cross
Croft Michael	*Croft Myghal*	- Michael's croft
Croft Noweth	*Croft Noweth*	- New croft
Croft Pascoe	*Croft Pasco*	- Pascoe's croft
Croftow	*Croftow*	- Crofts
Crowgey	*Crowjy*	- Cottage, hovel
Crows-an-wra	*Crows an wragh*	- Witch's cross
Crugmeer	*Cruk-mur*	- Great mound or barrow
Crugoes	*Crugow*	- Barrows, mounds (Eng. plural's' added)
Crumplehorn	*Tremaelhorn*	- Maelhorn's farm
Cubert		- Saint's name
Culdrose	*Kyl ros*	- possible 'nook in the heath'
Cury		- from Corentyn, the parish priest
Cutcare	*Cos-ker*	- Wood or hill-fort
Cutcrew	*Cos-know*	- Nut wood
Cutmadock	*Cos-Madoc*	- Madoc's wood
Cutmere	*Cos-mur*	- Great wood
Cutparrett	*Cos-perveth*	- Inner or middle wood

Calenick (Nr. Truro)

18

D

Dannon	*Deu-nans*	- Two valleys
Darracott		- (Eng.) Dodda's farm
Degibna		- From chapel of St Degiman
Delabole		- From 'Delyow', stream or district name
Demelza	*Dyn-Melsa*	- Fort of Maeldaf
Dennis	*Dynas*	- Fort
Denzel		- Probably : Fort & personal name
Devoral		- Watery place
Devoran	*Devren*	- Wet valley
Dewey		- Common stream name (perhaps 'Goddess')
Dinas	*Dynas*	- Fort
Dizzard	*Dyserth*	- Retreat, wild place
Dobwalls		- (see Doublebois)
Dolcoath	*Dor coth*	- probably 'Long close'
Dollar Ogo		- Dollar Cave (Eng. order)
Domellick	*Dyn Maeloc*	- Maeloc's fort
Dorminack	*Dor-meynek*	- Stony ground
Dosmary Pool		- '-mary' is probably 'mere' (Eng.)
Doublebois		- Two woods (French)
Dowgas	*Deu-gos*	- Two woods
Downderry		- Probably Eng. meaning obscure
Dowran	*Dowran*	- Valley bottom
Draynes	*Dreyn*	- probably 'thorns' (Eng. plural 's')
Drewollas	*An dre-woles*	- The lower farm
Drift	*? An dref*	- Poss. 'The farm'
Drym		- Ridge
Duloe	*Dyw logh*	- Between the two (river) Looe (s)
Dunheved		- (Eng.) Down-head, head of downs
Dunmere	*Dyn mur*	- Great fort
Dupath		- Probably Eng. 'Thieves' path
Duporth	*Deu-borth*	- (Farm of the) two coves

19

Holy Well and Cross, St. Cleer

E

Eglaroose	*Eglos-ros*	- Church on heath or promontary
Egloshayle	*Eglos-heyl*	- Church on estuary
-kerry	*Kery*	- Church of St Kerry
-merther	*-merther*	- Church of burial place of saint
-rose	*-ros*	- Church on heath or promontory
Engelley	*An gelly*	- The grove
Engollen	*An gollen*	- The hazeltree
Ennis-vath	*Enys-Vargh*	- Mark's part of isolated land
Ennis-worgey	*Enys-Worgy*	- Gorgi's part of isolated land

F

Fentengoe	*Fenten-gok*	- Cuckoo's spring
Fentervean	*Fenten-vyghan*	- Little spring
Fentengollan	*Fenten-gollen*	- Spring of hazle-tree (or of Golan)
Fentongoose	*Fenten-gos*	- Spring of the wood
Feock	*Lanfeok*	- From parish saint
Fowey	*Fawwyth*	- 'Beechtrees' (name of river)
Fraddon		- poss. Small stream
Fursnewth	*Fos-noweth*	- New dyke

L ROWE.

Quethioc

Church

21

G

Gabbons		- Possibly : from 'Cam' - crooked
Gare	*An ger*	- Hill-fort
Garras	*Garow-ros*	- Rough heath
Gaverigan	*Gover-gwyn*	- White stream
Gazick	*An gasek*	- The mare
Gear	*An ger*	- Hill-fort
Geevor		- Possibly 'sunken road'
Gelly	*An gelly*	- Grove
Germoe	*Germogh*	- Name of parish priest
Gerrans	*Gerens*	- Name of Cornish king and saint (Gerent)
Gew (Graze)	*Gew gres*	- (Middle) close field
Gillan	*An gylen*	- Nook or creek
Gilley, Gilly (vean)	*An gelly vyghan*	- (Little) grove
Gilley, Gilly (Wartha)	*Wartha*	- Higher grove
Gloweth	*Glow-wyth*	- probably : Charcoal wood
Gluvian		- Name of parish saint
Godolphin	*Godolghen*	- probably : Little mound
Goenrounsen	*Gun-rounsen*	- Downs of the nag
Golant	*Golnans (Gwelnans)*	- Feast or field of the valley
Goldsithney	*Gol-sythny*	- Feast of Sithney
Goonamarth	*Gun an margh*	- Downs of the horse
Goon Bell	*Gun bell*	- Far downs
-goose	*gos*	- Wood downs
-gumpus	*gompes*	- Level downs
-havern		- Downs with fallowland
-hilly		- Briny (possibly 'hunting') downs
-hingey	*henjy*	- Downs of the old house
-hoskyn		- Hoskyn's downs
-laze	*las*	- Blue-green downs
-vean	*vyghan*	- Little downs
-vrea	*vre*	- Hill downs
Gormellick	*Gun-Maeiloc*	- Downs of Maeiloc (pers. name)
Gorrangorras	*Gun an gores*	- Downs of the weir
Goss Moor	*An gors*	- Marsh & Eng. moor

Govarrow	*Goverrow*	- Stream
Grampound	*Pons-mur*	- French 'Grand Pont'. Both names mean Great Bridge
Gratna		- Eng. for rough field
Greensplatt		- Eng. dialect for 'green place'
Greeb	*An gryb*	- Crest
Gregwartha	*Grug-Wartha*	- Higher barrow or mound
Gribba, Gribben	*An gryben*	- Small crest
Gue Graze	*Gew gres*	- Middle close, field
Gullaveis	*Gwel-a-ves*	- Far field
Gunnislake		- Probably : Eng. 'Gonna's stream or possibly connected with 'Gunnis' a worked-out part of mine.
Gunvena	*Gwyneneth*	- White hill
Gwarder	*Gwer-dhowr*	- probably Green water
Gwarnick	*Gwernek*	- Alder-grove or marsh
Gwarth-an-drea	*Gwartha an dre*	- Top of the town
Gwavas	*Gwafvos*	- Winter farm
Gwealavethan	*Gwel-avallen*	- Open cultivated field of the mill
-dues	-du	- Black field (Eng. plural 's' added)
-hellis	-Hellys	- Helston field
-mayowe		- Mayowe's field
-mellin	-melyn	- Mill field
Gwendra	*Gwyndre*	- White field
Gwendreath	*Gwyndreth*	- White beach
Gwennap	*Lanwenep*	- Name of parish saint
Gwinear		- Name of parish saint
Gwithian		- Name of parish saint
Gyllyngdune	*An gylen dhown*	- Deep nook or bay
Gyllyngvase	*An gylen vas*	- Shallow nook or bay

Talland Church, Nr. Looe.

H

Halabezack	*Hal wybesek*	- Moor of ? flies
Halamanning	*Hal-amanyn*	- Butter moor
Hallaze	*Hal-las*	- Green moor
Hallow	*Hallow*	- Moors
Halsferran	*Als-yffarn*	- Hell cliff
Halvana	*Hyr-veneth*	- Long hill
Halviggan	*?Gal-vyghan*	- Poss. small moor
Halwin, Halwyn	*Hal wyn*	- White moor
Halzaphron	*Als-yffarn*	- Hell cliff
Harlyn	*Har-lyn*	- Long lake
Harris, Harros	*Hyr-ros*	- Long heath
Harvose	*Hyr-fos*	- Long dyke
Hay	*Hay*	- Hedge or field
Hayle	*Heyl*	- Estuary
Hea	*Hay*	- Hedge or field
Hele		- (Eng.) Nook or angle
Heligan	*Helygen*	- Willowtree
Helland	*Hen-lan*	- Old holy place
Hellangove	*Hel-an-gof*	- Hall of the smith
Hellesveor	*Hellys-vur*	- Great 'Oldcourt'
Helligan	*Helygen*	- Willowtree
Helsbury	*Hellys*	- 'Old Court' & (Eng.) for hill fort
Helston	*Hellys*	- 'Old Court' & (Eng.) 'town'
Hendra	*Hendre*	- Old farm
Henforth	*Henforth*	- Old road
Hengar	*Hen-ger*	- Old hill-fort
Hennett	*Huthnans*	- Happy valley
Henver	*Hen-forth*	- Old road
Hernis	*Hyr-nans*	- Long valley
Herodsfoot	*Hyr-arth*	- Long yard & (Eng.) 'valley bottom'
Hessenford		- (Eng.) possibly 'Hag's ford'
Hewas	*Hewas*	- Summer pasture
Hole	*?Hal*	- Moor or (Eng.) hallow
Hor Point	*Pen-horth*	- 'Ram' Point
Hutnance	*Huth-nans*	- Happy valley

I

Illiswilgig	*Enys-welsek*	- Grassy island
Illogan		- Name of parish saint
Ince	*Enys*	- Island, isolated place
Indian Queens		- (Eng.) probably from inn sign
Irish		- Stubble (Eng. dialect)

J

Joppa	- Shop, blacksmith's shop

K

Karslake		- (Eng.) Cress-pool or stream
Keigwin	*Ke-gwyn*	- White hedge
Kellivose	*Kelly-fos*	- Grove of the dyke
Kellow	*Kellyow*	- Groves
Kelly (Bray)	*Kelly (Bre)*	- Grove (of the hill)
Kelynack	*Kelynek*	- Hollybushes
Kenegie	*Kenegy*	- Reed-bed, marshes
Kenidjack		- poss. place for gathering firewood
Kennegie, Kennegy	*Kenegy*	- Reed-bed, marshes
Kenwyn		- Name of parish saint
Kernick	*Kernyk*	- Nook or corner
Kerrow	*Kerrow*	- Camps, hill-forts
Kerslake		- Cress pool, stream (Eng.)
Kestle	*Kestel*	- Castle or village
Kilcobben	*Kyl-crom*	- Crooked nook. (Probably)
Killatown	*Kellyow*	- 'Groves' & Eng. 'town' or 'farm'
Killiganogue	*Kelly gnowek*	- ?Nut-bearing grove
Killigerran	*Kyl-Gerens*	- Retreat of Gerrans (St. and King)
Killigrew	*Kelly-gnow*	- Nut grove
Killiow	*Kellyow*	- Groves
Kilmarth, Kilmar	*Kyl-Margh*	- Retreat of Mark (or possibly 'horse)
Kynance	*Keynans*	- Ravine

L

Laddenvean	*An lan-vyghan*	- Little bank
Ladock	*Lasek*	- Name of parish saint
Laity	*Lety*	- Dairy ('milk-house')
Lamellion	*Nans-melyn*	- Mill valley
Lamellyn, Lamellyon	*Nans-melyn*	- Mill valley
Lanarth	*Lanergh*	- Clearing
Lancarrow	*Nans-carow*	- Stag valley
Land's End	*Pen an wlas*	- (Cornish with same meaning)
Landewednack	*Lansewynek*	- Holy enclosure of St Gwinwallo
Landlooe	*Nans-Logh*	- Valley of River Looe
Landreyne	*Nans-dreyn*	- Valley of thorns
Landrine	*Nans-dreyn*	- Valley of thorns
Laneast		- Holy place + personal name
Langdon		- Long hill (Eng.)
Langford		- Long ford (Eng.)
Lanhay	*An hay*	- The hedge (with both French & Cornish words for 'the')
Lanherne	*Lan-Hernow*	- Holy place of St Hernow
Lanhydrock	*Lanhedrek*	- Holy place of Hidroc
Lankelly	*Nans-Kelly*	- Valley of grove
Lanner	*Lanergh*	- Clearing
Lanseague	*Nans-tek*	- Fair valley
Lanseaton	*Nans-sythyan*	- Valley of Sythyan (Stream name that may mean 'winding')
Lanteague	*Nans-tek*	- Fair valley
Lanteglos	*Nans-eglos*	- Fair valley
Lantinning		- Holy place of St Yntennyn
La & Cornish words for 'the')		
Lanherne	*Lan-Hernow*	- Holy place of St Hernow
Lanhydrock	*Lanhedrek*	- Holy place of Hidroc
Lankelly	*Nans-Kelly*	- Valley of grove
Lanner	*Lanergh*	- Clearing
Lanseague	*Nans-tek*	- Fair valley
Lanseaton	*Nans-sythyan*	- Valley of Sythyan (Stream name that may mean 'winding')
Lanteague	*Nans-tek*	- Fair valley
Lanteglos	*Nans-eglos*	- Church valley

Lantinning		- Holy place of St Yntennyn
Lantewey	*Nans-dewy*	- Valley of River Dewy
Lanyon	*Lyn-yeyn*	- Cold pool
Launceston	*Lan-Stefan*	- Holy place of St Stephen + (Eng.) town
Leah	*Legh*	- Flat stone
Lee, Ley	*Legh*	- Flat stone (or Eng. 'lay field')
Lelant	*Lan-Anta*	- Holy place of St Anta
Leskernick		- ?Rocky ford
Lesnewth	*Lys-noweth*	- New court
Lesquite	*Lost-cos*	- 'Tail of the wood'
Lestoon	*Lost-un*	- 'Tail of the downs'
Lestowder	*Lys-Teudar*	- Court of (King) Teudar
Lewannick		- Holy place + personal name
Lewarne		- Holy place or valley of eldertrees
Lidcott, Lidcutt	*Los-cos*	- Grey wood
Linkinhorne	*Lankenhorn*	- Holy place of St Kenhorn (stressed in 'horn')
Liskeard	*Lyskerys*	- Court + personal name
Little Petherick	*Nans-fenten*	- Petherick is a late form of St Petroc, (Cornish means 'valley with spring')
Lizard	*Lys-arth*	- possibly 'High court'
Loe	*Logh*	- Sea-lake, estuary
Looe	*Logh*	- Sea-lake, estuary
Lostwithiel	*Lostwydhyel*	- probably 'Tail of Withiel (land named after its owner')
Ludcott	*Los-cos*	- Grey wood
Ludgvan	*Lusvan*	- Unknown, first part may be 'grey'
Luxulyan	*Lok-Sulyan*	- Cell, or holy place, of St Sulyan
Lydcott	*Los-cos*	- Grey wood

Morvah.

M

Mabe	Lan Vab	- Name of parish saint
Manders	Methros	- Middle of heath
Maen Du	Men du	- Black stone
Maen Lay	Men -legh	- Flat Stone
Maen Porth	Men Porth	- Stone of the cove
Magor	Magor	- Old walls, ruins
Maker	Magor	- Old walls, ruins
Manaccan	Managhan	- Minister
Marazanvose	Marghas an Fos	- Market of the dyke
Marazion	Marghas-vyghan	- Little market
Marketjew	Marghas (De) Yow	- Thursday market (Both Marazion and Marketjew came to mean the same settlement)
Mawgan		- Name of parish saint
Mawnan		- Name of parish saint
Meadrose	Methros	- Middle of heath
Mean Mellin	Men melen	- Yellow (or possibly 'mill') stone
Mean Toll	Men an Toll	- Holed stone
Medrose	Methros	- Middle of the heath
Mehal Mill	Melyn Vyghal	- Michael's mill
Mellan-coose	Melyn -gos	- Mill in the wood
Mellan-noweth	Melyn-noweth	- New mill
Mellan-vrane	Melyn-vran	- Crow mill (or mill of Bran (pers name)
Mellingey	Melynjy	- Mill house
Mellingoose	Melyn-gos	- Wood mill (i.e. 'in the wood')
Manaclidgey	Meneth-Closow	- Hill of hurdles
Manacrin	Meneth-Cryn	- Dry hill
Manadarva	Merther Derva	- Burial place of St Derva
Mena-dew(s)	Meneth du	- Black hill (sometimes with Eng. plural)
Mena-glaze	Meneth glas	- Blue-green hill
Mena-gwins	Meneth gwyns	- Windy hill
Men an Tol	Men-an-toll	- Stone with the hole
Man Aver	Men-an-avar	- Goat (or crayfish) stone
Menear	Men-hyr	- Long stone (from monument)
Menerdue	Meneth-du	- Black hill

30

Menhay	*Meneghy*	- Sanctuary (religious)
Menheniot	*Mahenyet*	- possibly Place (or sanctuary) of St Neot
Menherion	*Meyn-hyryon*	- Longstones (monument)
Menhyr	*Men-hyr*	- Long stone (monument)
Menkee	*Men-ky*	- Dog stone
Mennergwidden	*Meneth-gwyn*	- White hill
Mennaridden	*Meneth-reden*	- Hill of ferns
Men Par	*Men porth*	- Cove stone
Menwinnion	*Meyn-wynyon*	- White or blessed stones
Men-y-grib	*Men-an-gryb*	- Stone of the crest
Merrose	*Methros*	- Middle of the heath
Merther	*Merther*	- Burial place of saint (from 'Martyr')
Mesmear	*Mes-mur*	- Great field
Metherell		- Middle hill (Eng.)
Methrose	*Methros*	- Middle of the heath
Mevagissey	*Meva hag Ysy*	- 'Meva and Issey', the parish saints
Minack	*Meynek*	- Stony (field)
Minear	*Men-hyr*	- Lonstone (monument)
Mingoose	*Myn-gos*	- Edge of the wood
Molevenny	*Mol-veneth*	- Bare hill
Molingey	*Melynjy*	- Mill house
Molinnis	*Mol-enys*	- Bare island or isolated place
Mongleath	*Mengleth*	- Quarry or mine
Morvah	*Morvath*	- probably name of original parish saint
Mouls	*Mols*	- Wether, sheep
Mousehole	*Porth-enys*	- Eng. (Cornish means 'Island Cove')
Mulfra, Mulvra	*Molvre*	- Bare hill
Mylor		- Name of parish saint.

Corner in Polperro

N

Nancarrow	*Nans-carow*	- Stag valley
Nance	*Nans*	- Valley
Nancegollan	*?Nans-an-gollen*	- probably Hazeltree valley
Nance-loe	*Nans-logh*	- Sea-lake valley
Mance-mere	*Nans-mur*	- Great valley
Nance-trisack	*Nans-dreysek*	- Brambly valley
Nance-vallon	*Nans-avallen*	- Appletree valley
Nance-wrath	*Nans-an-wragh*	- Witch's valley
Nankelly, Nankilly	*Nans-Kelly*	- Grove valley
Nanpean	*Nans-byghan*	- Little valley
Nanscawen	*Nans-scawen*	- Eldertree valley
Nanscow	*Nans-scaw*	- Valley of eldertrees
Nansloe	*Nans-logh*	- Valley of sea-lake
-ladron	*Nans-ladron*	- Valley of thieves (may be corrupted from Lanhadron 'holy place of St Hadron)
-mellyn	*Nans-melyn*	- Mill valley
Nanteague	*Nans-tek*	- Fair valley
Nantrisack	*Nans-dreysek*	- Brambly valley
Nare	*An arth*	- The height
Newquay	*Towan Porth Lystry*	- (Eng.) Cornish = 'Sand-dune by ships' cove
Ninnes, Ninnis	*An enys*	- The island or isolated place
Noon Billas	*An-un-byllas*	- The downs of oats

O

Ogo Dour	*Ogo-dowr*	- Water Cave
Ogo Pons	*Ogo-pons*	- Bridge cave

P

Padjagarrack	*Peder-carrek*	- Four rocks
Padstow	*Lanwedhenek*	- Holy place of St Petroc (Eng.) The Cornish 'Lan' was dedicated to another saint, Guethenoc)
Panters Bridge	*? Pons Ihesu*	- If correctly identified, this was 'Jesus Bridge'
Par (Bean)	*Porth (Byghan)*	- (Little) cove
Parc-an-als	*Park-an-als*	- Field of the cliff
an Growes	*-an-grows*	- Field of cross
Bean	*byghan*	- Little field
Caragloose	*-Carrek-los*	- Field of the grey rock
Eglos	*-eglos*	- Church field
an Creet	*-an-cruk*	- Field of the mound or barrow
Park an Bowen	*Park-an-bowen*	- Beef field
an Castle	*-an-castel*	- Castle field
an Gear	*-an-ger*	- Hill-fort field
an Fold	*-an-fold*	- Field of the sheepfold
an Tidnoe	*-an-fentynyow*	- Field of the springs
Brauze	*-bras*	- Big field
Parkendillick	*Park-an-deylek*	- Field of the dung-heap
-en Gear	*-an-ger*	- Field of the hill-fort
-en Gew	*-an-gew*	- Field of the enclosure
Hoskyn		- Hoskyn's field
Uren		- Uren's Field
Venton	*an-fenten*	- Field of the spring
Parnvoose	*Porth-an-fos*	- Cove of the dyke
Pednandrea	*Pen-an-drea*	- End of the town
Pednanvounder	*-an-vownder*	- End of the lane or cattle-track
Pedn Brose	*-bras*	- Big headland
Pedn Men Du	*-men-du*	- Headland of black stone
Pedn Myin	*-meyn*	- End of the stones
-vadan	*-tal-van*	- Headland by the height
-y-ke	*-an-ke*	- End of the hedge
Penlean, Penlyn	*Penlyn*	- End of the lake
Pelynt	*Plu-Nynt*	- Parish of (Saint) Nent or Non
Penadlake, Penadlick	*Banathlek*	- Broom-brake

Pen-a-gader	*Pen-an-gadar*	- Headland of the chair
Penair	*Pen-arth*	- End of the heights
Pen-a-maen	*Pen-an-men*	- End of the stone or stones
-bothidna	*-buthynyow*	- End of the meadows
-bugle	*-bugel*	- Shepherds hill
-calenick	*-kelynek*	- End of hollybush grove
-carrow	*-carow*	- Hill of the stag
-coose	*-cos*	- End of the wood
-corse	*-cors*	- End of the marsh
-deen	*-dyn*	- Headland with fort
-dennis	*-dynas*	- Headland with fort
Pendoggett	*Pen-deu-gos*	- End of the two woods
-dour	*-dowr*	- End of the water or stream
-dower	*-dowr*	- End of the water or stream
-drea	*-an-dre*	- End of town
-enys	*-an-gelly*	- End of the island
-gelly	*-an-gelly*	- End of the grove
-gersick	*-an-gersek*	- End of the marshy place
-gilly	*-an-gelly*	- End of the grove
-glaze	*-glas*	- Blue-green head
-gover	*-gover*	- End of the stream
-hale	*-hal*	- End of the moor
-hallow	*-hallow*	- End of the moors
-halt	*-als*	- End of the cliff
Penhalvean, (-vear)	*Pen-hal-vyghan*	- (Great) or little 'End of the moor'
-hellick	*-helyk*	- End of the willow trees
-hole	*-hal*	- End of the moor
-kelly	*-Kelly*	- End of the grove
-kestle	*-Kestel*	- End of the castle or village
-lee	*-Legh*	- Headland of flat stones
-menor	*-meneth*	- End of hill
-nance, -nans	*-nans*	- End of valley
-nant	*-nans*	- End of valley
-nare	*-an-arth*	- End of the heights
-olva, -olver	*-an-olva*	- End of the lookout
Pennycomequick		- (Eng.) nickname for good field

Pennytinney	*Pen-fentynyow*	- End of the springs
Penpoll	*Pen-poll*	- End of pool
-ponds	*-pons*	- End of the bridge
-pont	*-pons*	- End of the bridge
-praze	*-pras*	- End of the meadow
-quite	*-cos*	- End of the wood
-ryn	*-ryn*	- End of the hillside
-rose	*-ros*	- End of the heath or promontory
Pentevale	*Pen-fenten-Fala*	- Source (springhead) of River Fal
Penstraze	*Pen-stras*	- End of the valley bottom
Pentire (Glaze)	*Pentyr-glas*	- (Blue-green) Headland
Pentreath	*Pentreth*	- End of the beach
Penventon	*Pen-fenten*	- head of the spring (source)
-ventine	*-fentynyow*	- Springheads
-vose	*-fos*	- End of dyke
-warne	*-an-wern*	- End of eldertrees or marsh
Penwith		- probably simply 'Extremity', 'End'
Penydevern	*pen-an-devran*	- End or head of the wet valley
Penzance	*Pen-sans*	- Holy head
Percuil	*Porth-cul*	- probably 'Narrow cove'
Perranarworthal	*Peran-ar-wodhal*	- Combination of two placesnames, one name after St Peran, the other possibly meaning 'On the thicket'
Perranuthnoe		- from Saints Peran and Guethenoc
Perranzabuloe	*Peran-treth*	- Peran (name of saint) in the sand : (Lat.) Cornish name identical in meaning
Petherwin		- Blessed Saint Padarn (parish saint)
Pigeon Ogo		- (Eng.) Pigeon + cave
Pill		- (Eng.) 'creek'
Pits Mingle	*Pyttys Mengleth*	- Quarry pits
Place	*Plas*	- Large house
Polangrain	*Pol-an-grun*	- Pool of the gravel
Poldew - dhu, - du	*Pol-du*	- Black pool
-gazick	*-an-gasek*	- Mare's pool
-glase, -glaze	*-glas*	- Blue-green pool
-gooth	*-goth*	- Goose pool
-gover	*-gover*	- Pool or end of stream

Pol -grain, -grean, -green	-grun	- Gravel pool
-hendra	-hendra	- Pool of the old farm
-higey	-heyjy	- Pool of the ducks
-kanoggo, -kanuggo	-cronogow	- Pool of toads
-kernogo	-cronogow	- Pool of toads
-kinghorne	-Kenhorn	- Pool of Kenhorn (pers. name stressed on 'horne')
Pollaughan	Poll-oghen	- Ox pool
Polmarth	Poll-margh	- Horse pool or Mark's pool
Pol-mear	Poll-mur	- Great pool
Polmennor	Pen-meneth	- End of hill
Polperro	Porth-pyra	- Cove + probably pers. name
Polpry	Poll-pry	- Clay-pit
Polridmouth	Porth-redman	- probably cove + pers. name
Polruan	Porth-Ruan	- Cove of Ruan (pers. name)
Polscatha	Porth-Scathow	- Pool (probably originally 'cove') of boats
Polstain	Poll-sten	- Tin-pit, tin-mine
Polstangey	Pons-Tangy	- Bridge of Tangey (pers. name)
Polstean, Polstein	Poll-sten	- Tin-pit, mine
-strong	-strong	- Dirty pool
-treworgey		- Treworgey Pool
-venten, -venton	-fenten	- Spring pool, or probably 'Head of spring'
-whele	-whyl	- poss. Pool of beetles
-wrath	-an-wragh	- Witch's pool
Ponjou	Ponsow	- Bridges
Ponsandane	Ponsan-den, Pons-an-deyn	- Either 'the man's bridge' or 'The dean's bridge'
Ponsanooth	Pons-an-woth	- Bridge of the goose
Ponsmain	Pons-men	- Stone bridge
Ponsmere	Pons-mur	- Great bridge
Ponsongath	Pons-an-gath	- Bridge of the cat
Ponsonjoppa	Pons-an-joppa	- Bridge of the smith's shop
Pont	Pons	- Bridge
Porn Boe	Porth-an-bogh	- Cove of the buck
Porthallow	Porth-Alow	- Cove of Alaw (pers. name)
Porthbean	Porth-byghan	- Little cove
-curno	-Kernow	- Cove of Curno (pers. name)

Porth -glaze	-glas	- Blue-green cove
-gwarra		- Cove + personal name
-gwidden	-gwyn	- White cove
Porthkea	Porth-ke	- Entrance to parish of St Kea
Porthledden	Porth-ledan	- Bread cove
-leven	-Leven	- Cove of St. Elvan (not 'leven' = calm)
-loe	-Logh	- Cove of sea-lake
-mear, meor	-mur	- Great cove
-mellin	-Melyan	- Cove of St Melyan
-nanven	-an-anvon	- probably 'Anvil cove'
-pean	-byghan	- Little cove
-scatho	-scathow	- Cove of boats
-towan	-towan	- Cove of sand-dune
Porth Holland	Porth-Henlan	- Cove of the old holy place
Port Isaac	-Yssak	- Cove + personal name, perhaps Isaac
Loe, Looe	-Logh	- Cove of the sea-lake
Mellon	-melyn	- Mill cove
Portreath	Porth-treth	- Cove on the beach
Port Quin	Porth-gwyn	- White cove
Port Scatho	Porth-Scathow	- Boats' cove
Praa (Prah)	Porth-an-wragh	- Witch or hag cove
Praze	Pras	- Meadow
-an-beeble	Pras-an-bybel	- Meadow of the ? pipe
-gooth	-goth	- Goose meadow
ruth	-ruth	- Red meadow
Predannack (Wollas)	Pen-redenek (woles)	- (Lower) Headland of fern-brake
Pridden	Pen-ryn	- Head or end of hillside
Prideaux		- French 'By the water'
Probus	Lan Brobes	- Name of saint

Quethiock		- Name of saint (just possibly Cadoc)
Quillets		- Small fields (Eng. dialect)
Quintrell Downs		- from personal name
Quoite		

38

Restormel Castle

R

Raginnis	*Ragenys*	- Facing the island
Rame		- Prob. Cornish word of unknown meaning
Ranneys		- Washing rocks (probably from 'ran' dialect for 'run', sea running over them)
Readymoney		- probably personal name, or (possibly) 'stone ford'; same name is in Polridmouth
Redannack, Redannick	*Redenek*	- Fern-brake
Redruth	*Res-druth*	- Ford + 'druth', meaning unknown: almost certainly *not* 'Red ford'
Reen(s)	*Ryn*	- Hillsides
Rescorla	*Res-corlan*	- Ford of sheepfold
Resparva, Resparveth	*Res-perveth*	- Middle of inner ford
Respryn	*Res-bryny*	- probably 'crows' ford'
Restronguet	*Restronges*	- Heath, second part of unknown meaning
Resugga	*Res-Ogo*	- Pos. Ford of the cave
Resurrance	*Res-Erens*	- Ford of Gerens (personal name)
Retallack, Retallick	*Res-Talek*	- Ford of Talek (pers. name)
Retire	*?Res-hyr*	- possibly 'long ford'
Rinsey	*Rynjy*	- probably 'House on hillside'
Rissick	*Res-segh*	- probably 'Dry ford'
Roche	*Tre-garrek*	- Rock (French); Cornish name 'Rock Farm')
Roose	*Ros*	- Heath
Roscarrock	*Ros-carrek*	- Heath of rock (at Budock: Cadoc's heath)
Roscroggan	*Ros-crogen*	- Heath of limpet shell
Roscrowgey	*Ros-crowjy*	- Heath of hovel
Rose	*Ros*	- Heath or promontary
Rose-an-growse	*Ros-an-grows*	- Heath of cross
Rosecare	*Ros-ker*	- Heath of hill-fort
Rosecraddock	*Res-Caradek*	- Caradoc's ford; this name is the Ridcaradoch in Geoffrey of Monmouth
Rose-in-vale, valley etc.	*Ros-an-avallen*	- Heath of the apple-tree
Roseland	*Ros*	- Promontory + Eng. 'land'
Rosemellin, Rosemellyn	*Ros-melyn*	- Mill heath
-manowas	-*menowes*	- Heath of awl (apparently)

Rose-modress	-Modres	- Modred's heath
-vean	-vyghan	- Little heath
-vear	-vur	- Great heath
-wearne	-wern	- Heath of alders or marsh
-win	-wyn	- White heath
-worthy	Res-worgy	- Ford + personal name
Roskear	Ros-Ker	- Heath of hillfort
-killy	-kelly	- Heath of grove
-pannel	-banathel	- Heath of broom
Rowden		- Rough hill (Eng.)
Ruan Lanihorne		- Ruan, saint's name and Lanihorne, 'holy place of Ryhorn'
Ruthdower	Ruthdowr	- Red water
Ruthvose	Ruthfos	- Red dyke

S

Saint Blazey	Landreth	- Cornish names means 'Holy place on beach'
Dennis	Dynas	- The word meaning hill fort was mis-identified as the saint
Erney		- Actually St Terney
Ingunger	Stum-gonger	- First part means 'bend'
Ives	Porth Ya	- The saint was called Ia (or Ea) : Cornish means 'Cove of Ia'
Levan		- The true name of the saint was Selevan
Sancreed	Sancres	- Name of saint
Savath	Enys Vargh	- 'Island', isolated place belonging to Mark.
Saveock	?Syvyek	- poss. 'strawberry patch'
Scarrabine	Roscarrek Bygham	- Little Roscarrock (see Roscarrock)
Sconner	Ros-Conor	- Heath of Conor (personal name)
Scorrier	Scorya	- Cor.: meaning unknown
Seaton	Sythyan	- Name of river (means 'twisting')
Sennen		- Name of parish saint
Sheviock		- poss- poss. slope'
Sithney		- Name of parish saint
Skewes		- Shelter
Skewjack		- Sheltered place

CPN-D

Skillywadden		- Possibly, 'Poor nooks'
Slade		- (Eng.) Shallow valley
Sparnick	*Spernek*	- Thorn-brake
Sparnon	*Spernen*	- Thornbush
Spernen Wyn	*Spernen wyn*	- Whitethorn-bush
Splatt		- Eng. dialect 'Plot'
Splattenridden	*Splat-an-reden*	- Plot of ferns
Stampas Farm		- from tin-stamps (mining machinery)
Stamps and Jowl Zawn	*Saun Stamps-an-jawl*	- Cleft of the devil's stamps (see above)
Stanbury		- Stone hill-fort (Eng.)
Stenalees	*Stenak-lys*	- Tin-ground in mud
Stencoose	*Stum-cos*	- Bend of the wood
Stennack	*Stenak*	- Tin-ground
Stephengelly	*Stum-an-gelly*	- Bend of the grove
Sticker		- probably word meaning 'stile'
Stithians		- Name of parish saint
Streetangarrow	*?Stret Garow*	- probably 'Rough Street'
Streetanowan	*Stret-an-avon*	- River street
Street-an-pol	*Stret-an-poll*	- Street of the pool
Strickstenton	*Tre-Gostentyn*	- Farm of Constantine

T

Talland	*Talan*	- Name of parish saint
Talvan(s)	*Tal-van*	- Next to the heights
Tal-y-maen	*Tal-an-men*	- Next to the stone
Tamsquite	*Stum-cos*	- Bend of the wood
Tehidy		- possibly 'House of retreat'
Temple		- from Knights Templar who owned church
Tideford		- Ford of River Tidy (Tiddy)
Tintagel	*Dyndajel*	- Fort + ? personal name

Tolcarne	Tal-carn	- Next to rock-pile
-garrick	-garrick	- Next to the rock
-gus	-gos	- Next to the wood
-pednpenwith	-pen-penwyth	- Next to the end of Penwith (qv)
-ponds	-pons	- Next to the bridge
Tolskiddy, Tolskithy		- Cor. meaning unknown
Tolvadden, Tolvan	Talvan	- Next to the heights
Tor		- (Eng.) 'rocky hill'
Torleven	Tre-leven	- Farm of Levan or Elvan (pers. name)
Torpoint		- (Eng.) 'Tail point'
Towan	Towan	- Dune
Towednack		- Name of parish saint
Trago	Tre-yago	- Farm of Iago
Trannack	Trevranek	- Farm of Branoc

Place-names beginning TRE are most often completed with a corrupt form of the name of the settlement's founder. (See BOS). Below are a few with old forms of these personal names.:

Treave -	*Farm of*	Yuf
Trebetherick		Petroc
Trefingey -		Brenci
Tregaddick, - dock -		Cadoc
Tregadjack -		Cadoc *or* Caradoc
Tregassick -		Cadoc
Tregellest -		Celest
Tregenna -		Ceneu
Tregonning -		Conan
Trehaverne -		Gafran
Treisaac -		Isaac
Trelew -		Lew
Treloweth -		Leuueth
Tremellick -		Maeiloc
Tremodrett -		Modred
Trenithen		Neithen
Trennick -		Uuethenoc, Guethenoc
Treringey -		Brenci
Tresaddern -		Sadorn

Treseder -	Seder
Tresillian -	Sulien
Tresulgan -	Sulcaen
Trethevey, Trethevy, Trethewey -	Dewi
Trethowell -	Dywel
Trevail -	Mael
Trevannion -	Ennion
Trevarthen, -ian -	Arthien
Trevaskis -	Maelscuet
Trevassack -	Madoc
Trevedras -	Modret, Medrawt
Treverbin -	Erbin
Trevecca -	Becca
Treverbyn -	Erbin
Trevilley -	Beli
Trevillick -	Maeiloc
Trevithick -	Budoc
Trevollard -	Maelvargh *or* Aelward
Trevorrick -	Uuoroc *or* Moroc
Trewarthenick -	Uyethenoc, Guethenoc
Treweatha -	Uuethen
Trewinnick -	Uuinoc, Gwynoc
Trewirgie -	Uuithci, Gwithgy
Trewithen -	Uuethen, Vueithen
Trewollack -	Uualoc
Treworgans -	Uuorcant, Gorgant
Treworgey -	Uuorci, Gorgy
Treworrick -	Uuoroc

Plen an Gwary, St Just.

L. ROWE.

Treath (Helford)	*Treyth*	- Passage (ferry)
Trebarvah, Trebarvath	*Treberveth*	- Inner or middle farm
-beigh	*Tre'n,byghan*	- Little farm or farm of man called An Byghan (Little)
-biffen	*-byghan*	- same as above
-bowland	*'n bowlan*	- Farm of cow-pen
-bray, brea	*bre*	- Farm on hill
-carne	*carn*	- Farm by rock-pile
-darrup		- probably farm by oaks
-dinnick	*Tredhynek*	- usually probably 'Fortified farm' (at Newlyn East: Farm in ferns)
-downs		- probably (Eng.) 'at the down'
-drea	*-dre*	- 'Home farm'
-drizzick	*-dreysek*	- Brambly farm
Treen	*Tre-dhyn*	- Farm at fort
Treforda		- probably (Eng.) 'at the ford'
-ffry	*Tre-fry*	- Upper farm
-gairewoon	*-ger-un*	- Farm by the hill-fort on the downs
-gantle	*Arghantel*	- Silver stream
-garden	*-gerdhen*	- possibly Farm by mountain ash or else farm + pers. name
-garland	*-gorlan*	- Farm by sheepfold
-garrick	*-garrek*	- Farm by rock (in St Cleer : Cadoc's Farm
-garthen	*-gerdhen*	- Farm by mountain ash, or else farm + pers. name
-gear	*-ger*	- Farm by hill-fort
-gerthen	*-gerdhen*	- see Tregarthen
-gew	*-gew*	- Farm by enclosed field
-goose	*-gos*	- Farm by wood
-goss	*-gors*	- Farm by marsh
Treheath		- (Eng.) 'At the heath'
Trehill		- (Eng.) 'At the hill'
Treheer	*Tre-hyr*	- Long farm
-lanvean	*-lan-vyghen*	- Farm by the little holy place (or bank)
-lawarren	*-lowarn*	- possibly Fox farm, or else Farm + pers. name
-lay	*-legh*	- Farm of the flat stone
-loan	*-lowen*	- Happy farm, or of someone callen Lowen
-loarth	*-lowarth*	- probably Farm of the garden

Tre-loyhan	-Tre-leghyon	- ?Farm of flat stones
-main, mayne	-meyn	- Farm of stones
Trembath	Tre'n bath	- Farm of the nook
-bleath	-blyth	- Farm of the wolf
-braze	-bras	- Farm of man called An Bras (Big)
-broath	-brogh	- Farm of the badger
Tremeer	Tre-vur	- Great farm
-menheere	-an-men-hyr	- Farm of the longstones
-methick	-an-medhek	- Farm of the doctor
Trenance	Tre-nans	- Valley farm
-nant	-nans	- Valley farm
-ncrom	'n - crom	- Valley of the curved hill
-nean	'n - en	- Valley of the lambs (or pers. name)
-near, -neere	'n - yer	- Valley of the hens (or pers. name)
-neglos	'n - eglos	- Valley of the church
-newth	-noweth	- New farm
-ngove, -ngrove	'n - gof	- Farm of the smith (or pers. name An Gof = Smith)
-nithan	'n - eythen	- Farm of the gorse, but probably Farm of Neithan, (pers. name)
-noon	'n - un	- Farm on the downs
-nouth	-noweth	- New farm
-nowah, -nower	-noweth	- New farm
-noweth, -nowth	-noweth	- New farm
Trentinney -	'n fentynyow	- of the springs
Trenwheal -	'n whel	- of the mine
Trenwith -	Trevenwyth	- of the elm-trees
Trequite -	Tre'n cos	- of the wood
Trereen Dinas -	Tredhyn Dynas	- Farm of the fort : contains two words meaning 'fort'
Trerice -	Treres	- Farm of the ford
-rose -	-ros	- Farm on the heath
-sawsan, -sawsen, -sawson	-sawson	- Farm of the English
-scowe	-scaw	- Farm of the eldertrees
Treslay, Treslea	Ros-legh	- Heath or promontory of flat stone
Tresmarrow	Ros-Margh	- Heath or promontory of Mark
Tresparrett	Ros-perveth	- Middle or inner heath

47

Trevarrack	Tre-varrek	- ?Knight's farm
-vean	-vyghan	- Small
-vear	-vur	- Great
Treveglos	Treveglos	- Churchtown
Treven		- (Eng.) At the fen
Trevenna	Treveneth	- Hill farm (At Mawgan. Elsewhere probably personal name)
Treviglas	Treveglos	- Churchtown
Trevisquite	Trevyscos	- Farm below wood
Trevose	-fos	- Farm at dyke
Trew	-dhu	- (In Breage) Black farm
Trewartha	-wartha	- Upper farm
-wavas	-wavas	- Farm at winter pasture
-wen, -win	-wyn	- White farm
-withen	-wedhen	- Poss. 'Tree farm'
-woof	-wof	- Farm of blacksmith
-woon	-un	- Farm of downs
-zance	-sans	- Holy farm
Trinnick	Tre-frynk	- Frenchman's farm
Trungle	Tre-vengleth	- Farm by quarry
Troon	Tre-un	- Farm on downs
Truro	Truru	- Early forms (Triweru)-(cannot be interpreted).
Trusell, Trussall	Tre-wystel	- Farm of the hostage (Prob. personal name)
Tucoyse	Tu-cos	- Side of the wood
Turnaware	Cores-Turnan	- Weir of Turnan (pers. name)
Tywardreath	Chy-war-dreth	- House on the beach or strand
Tywarnhayle	Chy-war'n-heyl	- House on the estuary

U

Liskeard Church

V

Valley Truckle	*An Velyn drukkya*	- Tucking mill (wool treatment)
Vean	*-Vyghan*	- Little (1st part of name missing)
Vear	*-Vur*	- Great (first part of name missing)
Vellangoose	*An velyn-goo*	- The mill in the wood
Vellanoweth	*An velyn-noweth*	- The new mill
Vellyndruchia	*An velyn-drukkya*	- Tuckingmill (wool treatment)
Vellynsaundry	*Melyn-Saundry*	- Saundry's mill
Venn		- (Eng.) 'fen', marsh
Venton (Ariance)	*Fenten Arghans*	- Spring (of silver)
Venton Ladock	*Fenten Lasek*	- Well or spring of St Ladock
Venton Raze	*Fenten Ras*	- Well or spring ? of grace
Venton Veor		- possibly 'great spring', but there may be a personal name attached
Ventonwyn	*Fenten-wyn*	- White well or spring
Veryan		- Name of parish saint
Vogue	*Fok*	- Furnace
Voose	*An Fos*	- The dyke
Vorrap Zawn	*Saun Vorrep*	- Cleft at seaside (Eng. order)
Vounder	*An vownder*	- Lane or cattletrack

W

Warleggan		- Probably a river name
Water-ma-trout		- probably (Eng.) 'Water (Wet) my throat', nickname for difficult field ?
Week St Mary		- Village of St Mary
Wendron		- from Gwendern name of parish saint
Wheal Alfred		- Alfred mine
Wheal Bal	*Wheal-Bal*	- Mine works
Wheal Basset		- Basset mine (name of mineral Lord)
Wheal Kitty		- Kitty's mine
Wheal Rose	*Whel ros*	- Mine on heath
Windsor, Winsor		- Usually (Eng.) Wind's edge

Witheven		- (Eng.) Withie fen
Withielgoose	*Gwydhyel-gos*	- Part of Withiel parish (named after patron saint) in wood
Withnoe		- probably from personal name Guethenoc
Woon	*An un*	- The downs
Woon Gumpus	*An un gompes*	- Level downs
Wra	*An wragh*	- the witch or hag

Y

Yeat (e), Yetta	*Yet*	- gate (Cornish from Old English)

Z

Zawn a Bal	*Saun an bal*	- Cleft of the mine
Buzz and Gen	*Saun Bosankan*	- Bosankan cleft
Reeth	*Reeth*	- Red cleft
South	*Soth*	- South cleft
Varrap	*Vorrep*	- Seaside cleft
Vinoc	*Veynek*	- Stony cleft
Zelah	*Seghla*	- Dry place
Zennor		- from St Senor
Zone Point	*Pen Saun*	- headland of the cliff

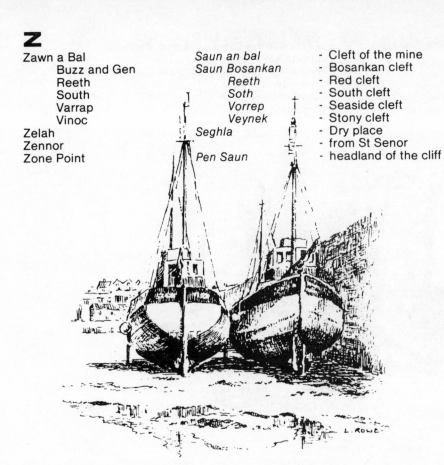

Fishing Boats, St. Ives.

Cornish Publications

Dyllansow Truran, Trewolsta, Trewirgie Hill, Redruth.
Tel.: Redruth 216796

CORNISH NAMES FOR CORNISH HOMES - *by Crysten Fudge, M.A.*　　9506431 0 6

A name-it-in-Cornish handbook, delightfully illustrated by Laura Rowe.　　95p

THE LIFE OF CORNISH - *by Crysten Fudge*　　C/C 0 907566 20 0
H/C 0 907566 24 3 H/C

The Story of our language to the 17th Century. An immensely scholarly and readable work. Attractively illustrated. A fascinating story told with the insight and understanding of a foremost Celtic scholar.　　Card Cover　£1.20
Hard Cover　£3.50

NAMES FOR THE CORNISH -　　0 907566 03 0

300 Christian names for your children - all of them Cornish. With derivations and translations.　　£1.20

A HANDBOOK OF CORNISH SURNAMES - *by G. Pawley White*　　9506431 9 X

Dr. A. L. Rowse points out in his foreword, the study of Cornish surnames is an essential work in the elucidation of the distinct Cornish identity.

KERNEWEK MAR PLEK !

The newest course in Cornish that has already revolutionised Cornish Language teaching.

KERNEWEK MAR PLEK - First Course - *by Crysten Fudge and Graham Sandercock*　　9506431 2 2
£1.95

Kernewek Mar Plek - Second Course - *by Crysten Fudge*　　9506431 5 7
£2.40

Cassettes available, convert this series into a home tuition course. For students of all ages.

CORNISH SAYINGS, SUPERSTITIONS AND REMEDIES - *by Kathleen Hawke.*   0 907566 04 9

"What makes Mrs. Hawke's work on dialect particularly interesting is that she has lived
for many years in both mid-Cornwall and West-Cornwall" K. C. Phillips.   90p

CORNISH QUIZ - *by R. S. Best.*   9506431 4 9

Over 500 questions and answers on Cornwall and things Cornish.   Illustrated by
C. M. Pellowe.   95p

A ST. PIRAN MISCELLANY - Kemysk Sen Perran - *by Brian Webb.*   0 907566 44 8

The stories and traditions of Cornwall's Patron Saint.   Told in Cornish and in English.   75p

CORNISH FAIST - *by Beryl James (first Lady Mayor of St. Ives).*   9506431 3 0

A book of dialect stories, including her Gorseth Kernow winning entries.   Illustrated by
Laura Rowe.   £1.00

CORNISH EPITAPHS Vol. I - *by John Keast*   0 907566 15 4

Records, humour, pathos and sermons in stone !   Beautifully illustrated with
photographs, line-drawings, etc.   This is volume one of a two-volume work.

Card Covers   £1.65

VISITORS TO CORNWALL - *by Ida Procter.*   P/B 0 907566 27 8
H/B 0 907566 26 X

As J. C. Trewin says in his Introduction - "Ida Procter can recreate her guests most
surely... Everyone is here; Francis Kilvert for example, Celia Fiennes is here - at St.
Austell.   Nearly two centuries later the young Beatrix Potter was arriving by train at
Falmouth.
It is an enchanting book"   Paperback   £3.50
Hardback   £5.95

CORNISH BEDSIDE BOOK No.1 - *by John Keast.* 9506431 8 1

Place-names, customs, dialects, remedies and recipes are nicely balanced by short essays and stories by early travellers, historical events and extracts from diaries. A thouroughly entertaining book. Card Covers £1.65

THE BOUNCING HILLS - Dialect Tales and Light Verse - *by Jack Clemo.* C/C 0 907566 38 3
H/C 0 907566 39 1

Jack Clemo says "I contributed many dialect tales to Cornish Almanacks before the war capturing the lighter side of Clay country village life as it was 50 years ago. I have chosen eight of these stories, and have added a selection of my comic verse (not in dialect, but with a Cornish flavour). There are about 20 short poems, mostly written for or about children".

This is a book from a Cornish literary giant shedding a new light on Cornwall's own blind poet. Card Covers £3.65
Hard Covers £6.75

ST. IVES HERITAGE - *by Lena & Donald Bray.* H/B 0 907566 07 3
C/C 0 907566 08 1

Recollections and records of St. Ives, Carbis Bay and Lelant. "This patient, well researched and loving look at history, customs and general lifestyle of this jewel of the North Cornish Coast makes this an unusually endearing narrative". Western Morning News. Hard Covers £4.95
Card Covers £2.95

THE HISTORY OF FALMOUTH - *by Dr. James Whetter.* H/B 0 907566 01 4
C/C 0 907566 02 2

The author's considerable knowledge of life in the 17th Century Cornwall provides much new information about the origins of the old town - its growth over three and a half centuries and its social, cultural and religious history. Hard Covers £4.95
Card Covers £2.95

MEMORIES OF OLD PENRYN - *by the late Florence Rapson.* 0 907566 42 1
Edited by Rita Tregellas Pope.

A picture of a way of life of which only nostalgic memories remain. £1.85

CARN BREA - *by Michael Tangye.*
C/C 0 907566 11 1

A book on Redruth, Illogan and Camborne's dominating feature. Michael Tangye's expert account will meet the needs of students of all ages and all of those who are curious about 'the Carn'. Illustrated by the author.

Card Covers £1.95

AROUND HELSTON IN THE OLD DAYS - *by A. S. Oats.*

A welcome re-issue of this popular title, first published 30 years ago. Described at the time of publication as "one of the most attractive books that can be added to a Cornish library, written by a Cornishman, full of love and knowledge of his own district and its history. His subjects range from prehistoric antiquities down to recent bygones and local humours."

£2.95

EARLY TIDE - *by Mary Lakeman.*

The late Mary Lakeman's enchanting evocation of the life as it was sixty years ago in the fishing village of Mevagissey. With a natural beauty of simple expression a fisherman's daughter has recreated this vanished world of colourful, local life and characters. First published by William Kimber in 1978.

£3.95

STATISTICAL ACCOUNT OF THE PARISH OF ST. JUST-IN-PENWITH - *by Rev. John Buller.*

This book, long sought after by scholars and antiquarian book collectors alike, is a fascinating account of life in St. Just 140 years ago. Natural history, geology, the mines, the building of the first lighthouse on the Longships in 1793, and the archaeological sites of which he says, quaintly, "the Druidical antiquary will visit with great interest." With foreword written for this fascimile edition by Peter Laws. Available in cased edition only.

£7.95

SAINT ENDELLION - *by Prebendary Edwin Stark.*

"The book is a learned piece of work and has been extensively researched. It will no doubt be greatly valued by all those who are interested in the many facets of Cornish history" . . . Western Morning News. The Author of this work about the saint, her church and Collegiate Foundation is at present Parish Priest of Blisland & St. Breward. In cased edition only.

£6.75